Yeppa Part V

We

Travel in the city

you can see

the beauty

the difference In language

and culture

that is the magic word

in the world

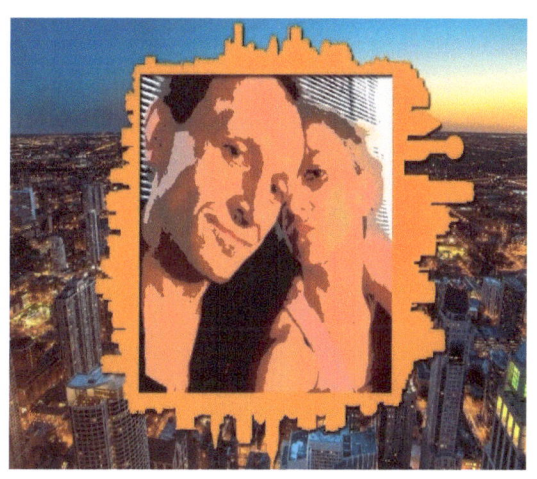

Dubai the first station

shows the relation

between the worlds

in own words

arabic language is not easy

the font is the key

Paris the town of love

a city to move

the feelings and more

and that is for

a precious moment

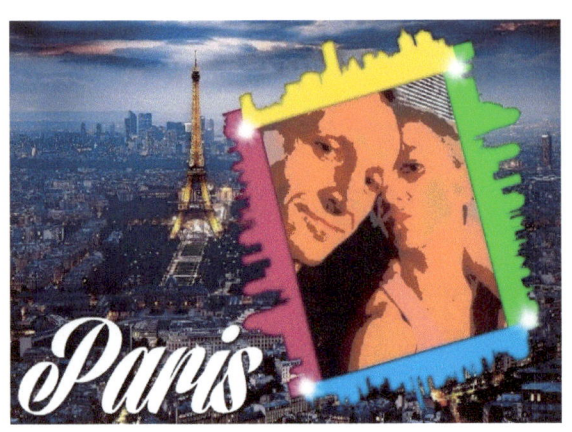

London the next trip

with the ship

the king, princes and

princess

more and less

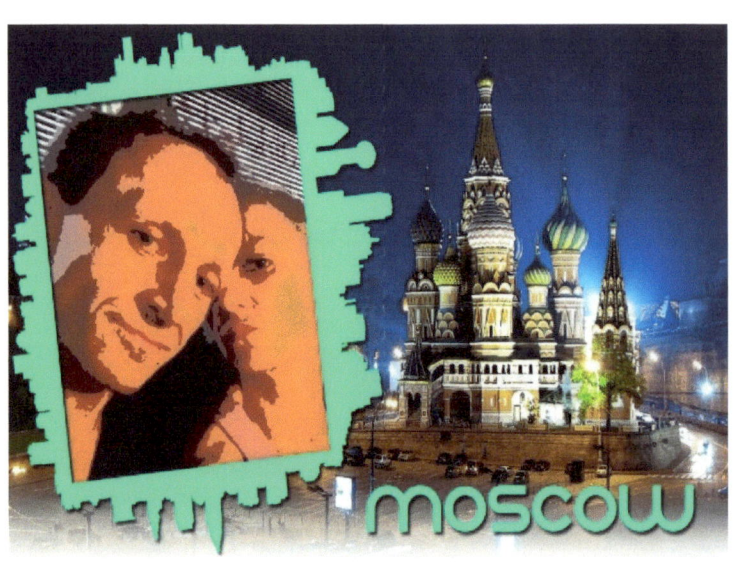

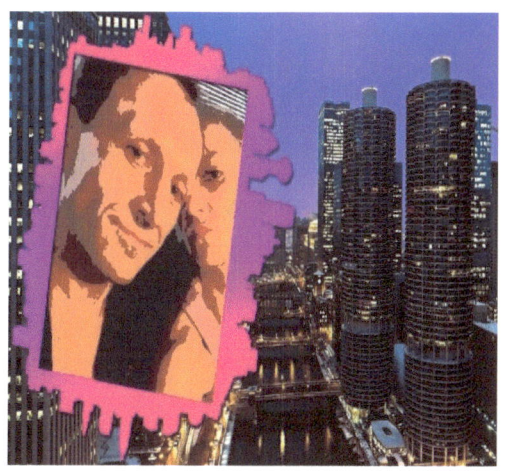

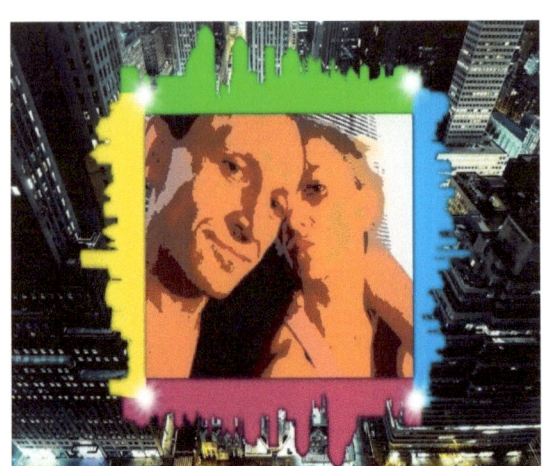

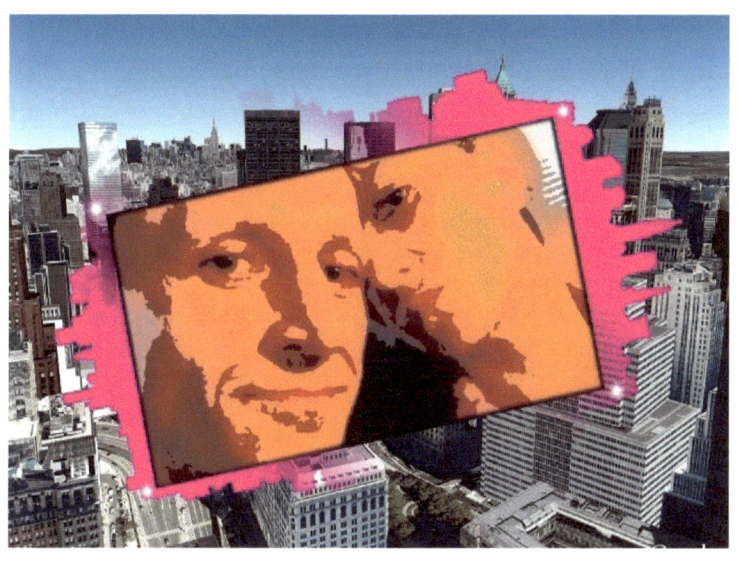

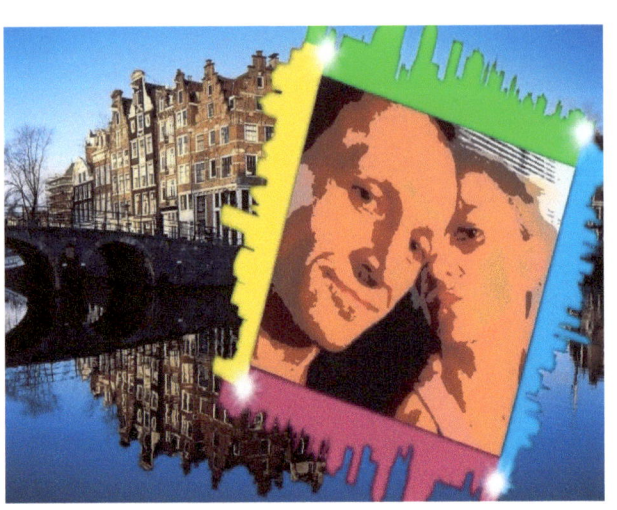

Travel from town to town

not to be down

to enjoy the sightseeing

being

a part of the global

thing

the knowledge around

listen to the sound

of the secrets

Action - to do a lot

to make a snapshot

to express the emotions

right in the moments

sing the song

nothing goes wrong

together with you

and to do

what is important

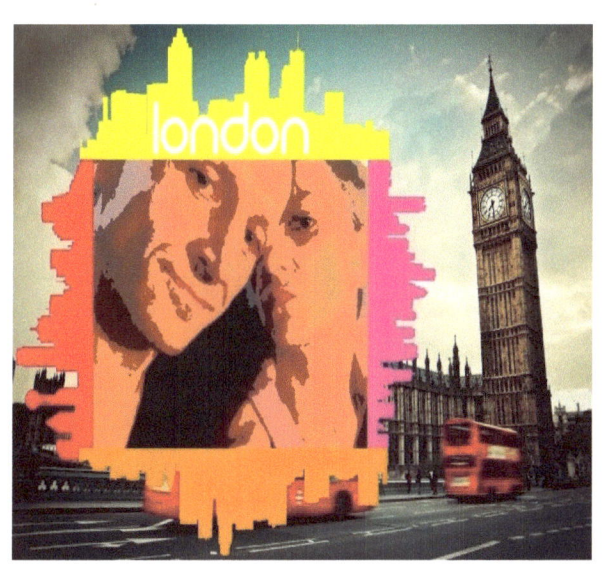

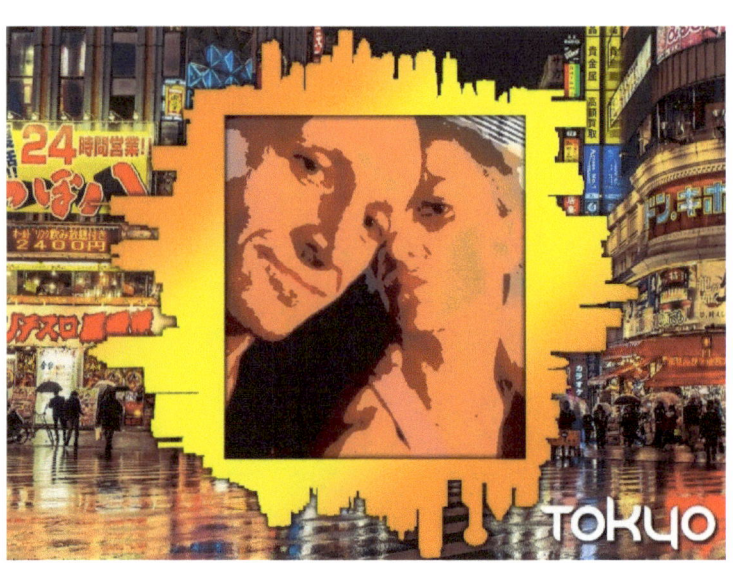

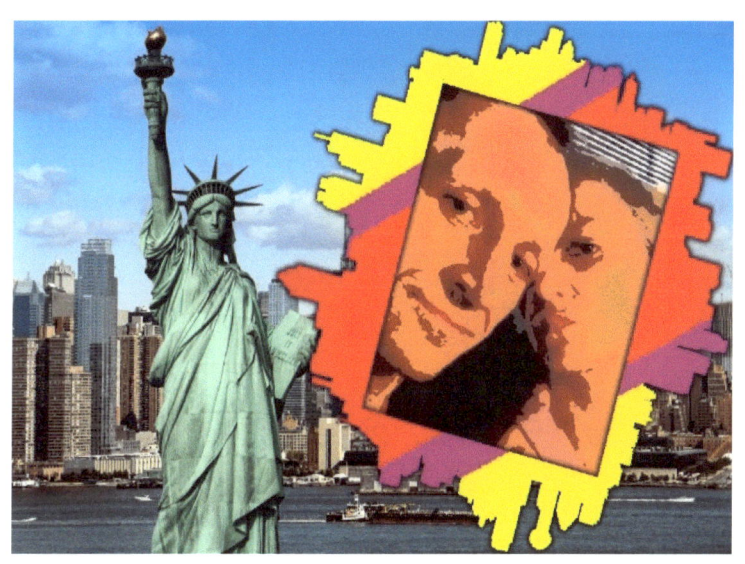

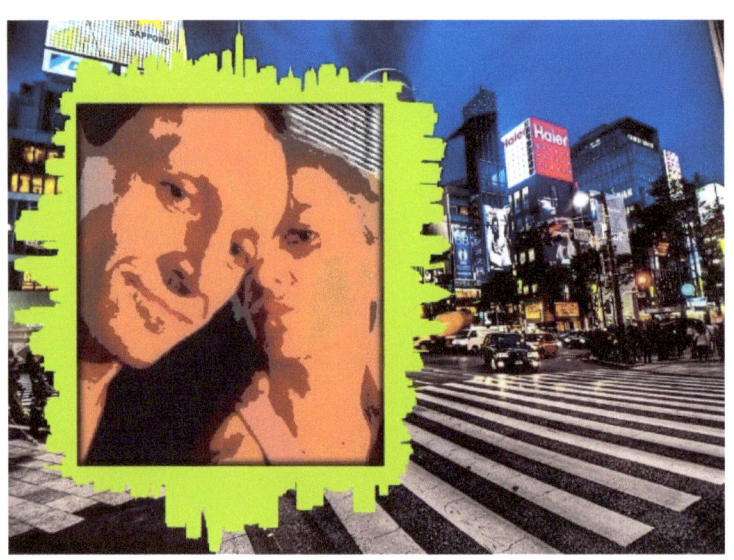

New York the strange

world

the   parts   of   a   great
nation

building the fascination

of so much sights

like

the wonderufl central park

shining bright in the dark

The point of silence

no reason for violence

the peace all around

in the middle of every town

will be reality

with the ability

to understand the same language

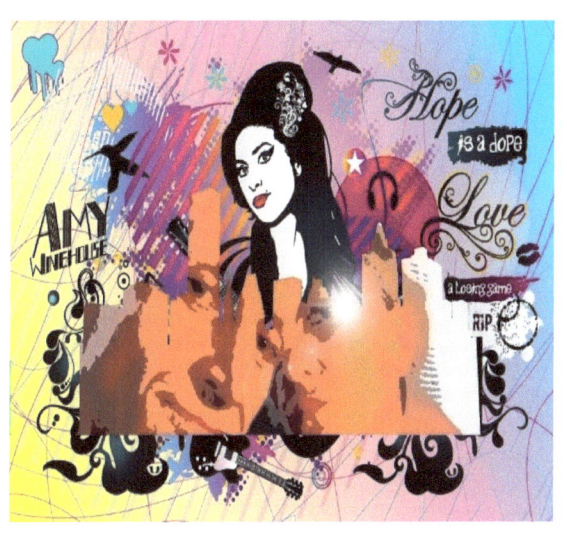

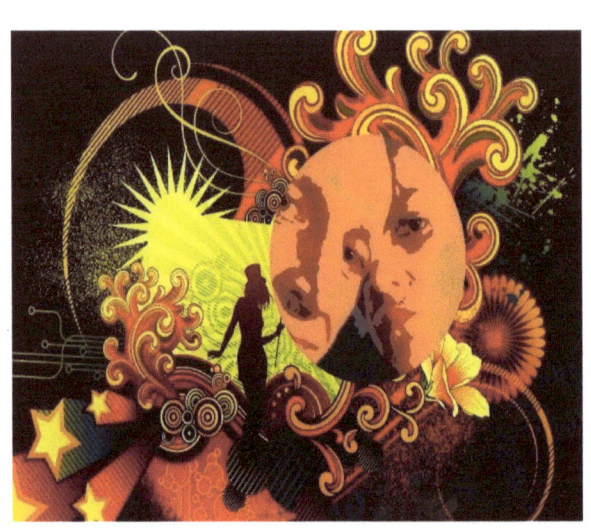

We say Yes to Yeppa!

www.ingramcontent.com/pod-product-compliance
Lightning Source LLC
Chambersburg PA
CBHW041623180526
45159CB00002BC/986